BECOME A
HOME-STAGER
TODAY!

NO EXPERIENCE?
NO PROBLEM!

A complete guide to owning & operating a
home-staging business

By: Karen Kelly, sds

DEDICATION

To all my fabulous students and fellow stagers: you make the world a *beautiful* place! Thank you for inspiring me.

ACKNOWLEDGEMENTS

Thanks to my biggest supporters--my husband, Ed, and my mom, Jane. The rest of my family rocks, too.

Thanks to Richard Calhoun who suggested the idea of becoming a stager and helped me get started.
(You can contact Richard at the following address: RichardCalhoun@CreeksideRealty.com)

To the realtor team of Sharon and Doug Keefer--thanks for all the work, your support, and your friendship.
(Contact the Keefers at www.SharonKeefer.com)

Thanks to Mike Willson who helped me publish this book--I couldn't have done it without him. Seriously.
(Visit Mike at www.CPRescue.com)

Thanks to Sara Aurich, who encouraged me for years to publish this book and then helped me improve it with her amazing editing. (For editing services, contact Sara at SaraAurich@comcast.com)

Thanks to my friends at Brook Furniture Rental for working with me to make my business a success.
(www.BrookFurnitureRental.com)

TABLE OF CONTENTS

WHO WOULD HIRE *ME?*

Several years ago, a real estate agent and friend asked me for some design advice on one of his listings. He told me about an intriguing new marketing strategy in real estate called "staging." He thought I would be a natural at it and that it might be a great career for me. I agreed. We did some brainstorming; he helped me get my first job and before I knew it, I had an exciting, new career.

When I started in the business, staging was a fairly new concept. During the first few years of my career, I spent a lot of time educating real estate agents and their clients about its values. However, there was no one to educate *me* on how to start and operate a staging business. I was quite nervous, actually. I couldn't imagine who would hire me. Even though I had some previous experience as a real estate agent, I had no formal training in interior design or decorating. I had no background or education in business. All I had was a passion for design and the belief that I could succeed. And guess what? I did. And so can you.

In the following pages, you will find easy step-by-step instructions on how to start and operate your own successful home-staging business. If you're looking for a well-paying part-time job with lots of flexibility, or if you're a real go-getter who wants a full-time career with the potential to earn some serious money, and if you *love* to decorate, staging is the perfect profession for you.

I was clueless when I started and had to learn many lessons the hard way. I'd like to save you that trouble. Armed with the following information, there is no reason you can't be out staging your first house right now. You know you want to. So, read on and *go for it!*

1

THE NUTS & BOLTS OF STARTING A HOME-STAGING BUSINESS

SELECTING YOUR BUSINESS NAME

First impressions are important, so a good business name and a beautiful business card are a must. Consider several possible names. Don't rush to make your decision. Run some of your choices by your friends and see which ones they like. If most of them like a particular name, pay attention—it might be the winner, even if it's not *your* favorite.

HELPFUL HINT

It's helpful if your business name lets your customer know at a glance what it is that you do.

As an example, let's consider...

Jane Smith's Staging Services

Not very exciting, but it's effective. Here's one thing I've learned. Real estate agents (who will provide most of your business) are extremely busy people. You'll lose their interest very quickly if you don't get right to the point.

In addition to a great business name, I like the idea of a motto--it helps people remember you. My company motto is "Stage It Well, Watch It Sell!"®. People may not remember my name, but they always remember my motto.

Once you pick your business name, you're ready to take care of a few more important steps.

FICTITIOUS NAME STATEMENT

If you're not using your personal name as part of your business name (as in the example above), it may be necessary for you to file a Fictitious Name Statement (FNS). An FNS is required by law so that consumers are able to connect the business name to the business owner. This is the same as "Doing Business As" or DBA. You'll need your FNS/DBA to open your business banking accounts.

To file, go on-line to your County Clerk Recorder's Office or do the following:

- Use the keywords *Fictitious Name Statement +* your city and state

and you'll find a website describing the requirements and the costs for your area. Some counties may not require an FNS. It's important to find out if yours does.

HELPFUL HINT

Search the website from the comfort of your own home to make sure that the name you've selected for your business is not already being used by someone else. Also be careful about using a name that's similar to another company name. If they don't run a reputable business, you wouldn't want to risk being confused with them and you certainly don't want their creditors coming after you!

Next:
- Print out a free application (if available on the website)
- Fill it in and send it off with a check (I paid $37.00 in my area)

Once your FNS has been filed, local newspapers will begin contacting you with offers to publish your FNS. Check their prices, pick the one you like, and send them a check (about $15.00 in my area). In my county, I was required to file my FNS before I began doing business (or within 40 days of my first transaction). Then I had to publish my FNS within 30 days of the filing.

Once that's done, it's off to apply for your business license.

BUSINESS LICENSE

Your business license is just a fancy name for a flat-rate business tax fee. You'll need to check the requirements and fees for your area and then pay up. You may be able to file on-line in your city or county.

I went to the Business License Tax Office at City Hall, filed my application, and paid the business license tax which, in my area, is $150.00 per year. Fees in your area may differ.

HELPFUL HINT

Use the keywords "how to file for a business license + your city and state" and learn how to file in your area.

TAX CLASSIFICATIONS

Keep in mind the following definitions are informal and meant only to help you decide which type of tax classification is best for you. What type of tax classification you declare for your business will determine what tax forms you submit, your personal liability regarding your business, and in some cases what type of write-offs you can declare.

Speaking with a professional tax accountant is highly recommended. If you can't afford an accountant at this time, there are many information sources available for free or a minimal cost. Here are some ideas:

- Visit the IRS website (www.usgov.gov).
- Make an appointment for a consultation (either in person or via the telephone with an IRS representative).
- Attend a course provided by the IRS (your local library and/or entrepreneur center can tell you when and where).
- Attend an adult education course on taxes.
- Contact SCORE (Service Corps of Retired Executives), www.score.org, or the Small Business Administration (SBA) www.sba.gov for classes and information. I found SCORE to be especially helpful when I started my staging business.

Sole Proprietorship

A sole proprietorship is usually owned by a single person. The owner operates the business and reports profits and losses on personal income tax.

General Partnership

Partnerships require an agreement between two or more people who own and operate a business together. The partners share profits, losses, and managerial duties, and each partner is personally liable for the partnership's debt. Partnerships file informational returns but don't pay partnership taxes. The individual partners report their share of the profits and losses on their personal returns.

Limited Liability Corporation (LLC)

An LLC will provide you the limited liability of a corporation and has the tax advantages of a partnership and sole proprietorship. Profits and losses are passed through the company to its "members". Its members are actually the owners, and the business can be run either by its owners or by appointed managers. LLCs can be taxed like a corporation, but they don't have stock and are less complicated to run than a Corporation.

STAGING STORIES

Not all staging jobs are as elegant and glamorous as you might think.

At the jobsite it's all about unpacking boxes, moving furniture, setting up house, hanging pictures, etc. It's often sweaty, dirty, dusty work.

Although it's not always glamorous, once in a while there are moments that are extra special.

A couple of summers ago, I was asked to consult with a customer at his home in a very affluent, upscale neighborhood. It was a high-end property and the job would look nice on my resume. The client was a very well-known and respected businessman in the area, and even a little bit "famous".

I didn't know this about him when I showed up at his home, but I had some suspicions about his status when he arrived a few minutes later...in a helicopter! Cooooool.

BUSINESS CARDS

Once you're happy with the business name you've selected and you've filed your FNS, order some business cards. You can't do much without a business card. Again, that busy real estate agent may only have time to say hello and ask for a card. Remember, your card is the first impression an agent, or any other potential customers, will have of you. You want it to be good.

Business cards don't need to be expensive, but they should look professional. Think about what image you'd like to portray. Do you have a sense of humor? Do you want your image to be elegant? Are you playful? Or are you more serious? You decide--it's up to you. It's O.K. to be clever but don't be too cute. You do want to be taken seriously.

HELPFUL HINT

It's easy to go on-line to the numerous websites that offer business card designs and printing. There are loads of designs to choose from and you can spend as little as $15 or $20 and still find some fantastic cards. Some companies even offer free business cards. My favorite resource is www.vistaprint.com. Register with your email address and take advantage of their great products, services, and discounts.

Initially, I wouldn't spend a lot because as you settle in to your new business, you may decide you'd like to modify your past choices. When you really feel like you've found your direction, you can opt for a more expensive and professional card. Once that happens, it's easy and fun to coordinate your stationery, greeting cards, and envelopes to your business card.

HOMEWORK FOR CHAPTER 1

Write down five possible business names (or as many as you can think of):

1.

2.

3.

4.

5.

Show them to your friends, but don't tell them which one you like the best and see which one they pick.

Once you've settled on a business name, go to www.vistaprint.com, register with your email address and begin looking at possible templates for your new business cards. This was, and still is, one of my favorite things to do.

HOW TO MEET CUSTOMERS

WHERE TO MEET YOUR CUSTOMERS

Once you have your wonderful, new business cards, you're ready to meet and impress your potential customers.

As I mentioned before, real estate agents are (in my opinion) your biggest source of business. It's rare that a homeowner will call me directly concerning staging. If they do, it's usually because their agent has advised them to do so. Most of my calls come from the agent themselves, and in many cases an agent will also be the one who finances the project. When working with real estate agents who are not already familiar with staging, you might want to explain how providing staging for their customers as part of their marketing package will make them look extremely savvy and a stand out from the competition. If the agent likes that suggestion, you'll be in a good position to join his team and offer your staging services to his future clients.

So where do you go to meet real estate agents? I was lucky that I had a friend who was also an agent, and as I said before, he was instrumental in helping me get my first job. If you're friendly with an agent, get them to help you. Ask if you can stage one of their listings. Ask them to introduce you to other agents. Give them a deal, buy them lunch, beg on bended knee, but get them to help.

If you don't have an agent friend, all is not lost. In fact, it's quite easy to meet all the agents you'll ever need by attending realtor marketing meetings in your area. In order to attend, it may be necessary for you to become an affiliate member of your local real estate board.   If so, here's how to do it:

- **Go on-line and use the keywords *Association of Realtors + (your state)*. Locate the board or association in your area.**
- See what requirements are necessary to become an affiliate member.
- Once you've paid any fees and met all other affiliate requirements, you should be eligible to attend all the realtor marketing meetings in your area. Join as many boards as you can and you will have access to hundreds of agents. Not only

can you find them, but now, through the board's website, they can find you as well.

It may not be necessary for affiliates to join the local real estate board in your area. But you should always find out what's expected of you to be eligible to attend realtor marketing meetings.

MARKETING MEETINGS

These are usually breakfast meetings held at a nearby restaurant where realtors meet to network with other realtors, vendors, and affiliates. There is usually a small charge for each meeting which pays for coffee and/or a small breakfast of some sort. If you're smart, you'll attend a marketing meeting every morning and meet as many people as you can. You need to be consistent and attend regularly. This is how people will get to know you. People have short memories. If you aren't present every week, you will soon be forgotten and a stager who *is* present every week will end up getting the work.

When attending any meetings, find out what the protocol is so that you don't inadvertently annoy someone by doing something wrong. You'll find that most meetings have similar formats, but some groups will allow you to do things that other groups won't. For example, at some meetings, you're invited to put your promotional materials on each table, but at other meetings you can't. So find out what's what.

In some cases, affiliates are given a quick chance to plug their businesses at each meeting.

HELPFUL HINT

I strongly suggest you prepare a 30 second "infomercial" about your business, and commit it to memory. I can't tell you how valuable it is.

Use the following to help get you started on your own presentation:

Hi. I'm _____ from _____. I offer quality staging services for the home you're about to sell or affordable redesign services for the home you live in now. If you're a real estate agent and you want your listing to sell faster and for a better price, I can help. Call me today at _____. Thank you.

Also consider creating a company motto or tag-line. A clever motto helps people remember you. It gives you a hook that another stager might not have. This is just a little something extra to help you stand out. Here's more on standing out...

At the marketing meetings, try to be a "standout," but only if you can do it without being obnoxious. Perhaps you can come up with a way of introducing yourself that's funny or clever in some way. Everyone likes to laugh and be entertained. Your colleagues are no different.

Here's a suggestion. I've done this at the realtor meetings before and it's always been a success.

I purchased two identical boxes of candy. I wrapped one box with brown paper and string and the other box with designer wrapping paper and curly ribbon. When it was my turn to introduce myself at the marketing meeting, I stood up and said, "Some of you may not understand the value or importance of staging. Let me explain." I then held up the plain box and said "This is your listing **without** staging." Then I held up the pretty box and said "and this is your listing **with** staging." That's about all I had to say, because everyone got the joke right away and they all had a good laugh. Next, I threw one box in one direction (with a warning to "catch") and then I threw the other box in the other direction. Two people got gifts from me that day (with my promotional materials tucked neatly inside) and everyone enjoyed my presentation. I didn't have to say much, which was a big relief, because public speaking is scary, but I made a big impact and many of the agents asked for my card after the meeting.

As an affiliate, you may also have the opportunity to sponsor some of the breakfast meetings, meaning that you buy some simple breakfast food for everyone (donuts or yogurt, for example), and in return you'll be allowed to give a short presentation about your business. It may cost you a hundred dollars or so to feed everyone (if you have a large group), but it may be worth it to have another chance for people to get to see you and learn about you and your company. At our meetings, the sponsor gets to keep all the business cards collected from the attendees. You can then use those names to start or add to your own mailing list.

HELPFUL HINT

I co-sponsored a breakfast meeting with a friend who has a professional organizing business. We thought our services were compatible and we decided to sponsor a meeting together and split the cost.

Following the breakfast meetings, there is often a "tour" of the houses for sale that the agents at the meeting are there to promote. Some of the agents and other affiliates will then caravan from house to house to preview each home.

It's a good idea to go on the tours with the agents. It's another way for them to get to know you. Don't drive by yourself, though. Try to hitch a ride with others so you'll have a chance to get some one-on-one time with a few of the agents. If you think it would be appropriate and not intrusive, you might even make some design suggestions to the agents representing each house. The tours move rapidly though, so don't keep anyone from getting on their way. It might be better to pick up the business card of that agent and contact them later.

As an affiliate, be the **best** affiliate you can be. Realtors are forever throwing parties, giving fashion shows, sponsoring golf tournaments, wine tours, charity drives, you name it. Join in. First of all, it's tons of fun and secondly, realtors *LOVE* affiliates that get involved and support their causes. For some real estate boards there's even an Affiliate of the Year award. Go for it! It's great for business and you'll have a wonderful time going to all the functions.

Another place to meet realtors and other affiliates is the Women's Council of Realtors (WCR) in your area. Don't let the name fool you. Men can be members of the WCR as well. There is a yearly fee required to join. Once you're a member, you're welcome to attend luncheons, volunteer for committee work, participate in fund raisers, etc., which will really give the realtors a chance to know you. Remember, realtors love affiliates that get involved and donate their time and energy to worthwhile causes.

You may consider joining a business networking group or "leads" club. Once again, you will be required to pay membership dues. I'm not convinced, however, that these clubs are the best place for you to network. Leads clubs, though fabulous for most entrepreneurs, only allow one member from each profession to join a chapter. You need to meet LOTS of real estate agents, not just one. So my advice would be, check out a leads club by attending once or twice as a guest, and see what you think. You might feel it's great for you. If so, by all means, join.

Check online, your local papers, or your Chamber of Commerce (also another great place to promote your business and which also requires a membership fee) to find networking mixers or get-togethers that you can attend. They're usually in the evenings or on weekends and you can meet lots of other entrepreneurs, do some networking, and exchange cards.

HELPFUL HINT

All these clubs and organizations have loads to offer, but not all of them are going to be right for you. Check them out and see what works best. While you are getting started in this business, I'd recommend you skip all the clubs and concentrate on meeting real estate agents. The realtor breakfast meetings will, in my opinion, give you the biggest bang for your buck.

Collect business cards from everyone you meet. If someone approaches you at one of these meetings and asks for your card, of course give it to them and ask for one of theirs. Then when you get back to your office, I suggest you sit down and hand-write a note telling them what a pleasure it was meeting them and that you're looking forward to working with them in the future, or whatever might be appropriate. I can't tell you how many notes I wrote when I was starting in this business (and still do). Everyone appreciates a personal note. It makes them feel special and it will make *you* more likable. Never underestimate the value of a hand-written note.

I write notes to express my appreciation for any help or favors I've received along the way. You should too. If you're not a good writer, you'll find some samples later (pg. 50) that you can tailor to fit your own needs.

HELPFUL HINT

Bring promotional materials to any and all of these meetings. It can be a simple flier that you printed on your own computer. Remember, try to make your message clear at one glance. See Appendix B for ideas.

The following seems like a good attention-getter, doesn't it?

What can you do to make your listing stand out from the competition?

It's intriguing, yes. But really…what does it mean? The purpose of the flier is not clear at first glance and now the reader has to spend more time studying it to see if it's something they're going to be interested in. Most likely, a busy realtor will not take the time to read on and you've lost your opportunity to have them pick up your flier. Instead, try something like this:

STAGING! IT SELLS REAL ESTATE!

Now that gets their attention! The reader then knows what your flier is about and whether or not they want to pick it up. I can almost guarantee they won't even bother with the first one. Go to Appendix B for some sample fliers.

If for whatever reason there are no breakfast meetings or leads groups or business networks to attend in your area, try starting a group of your own. If all else fails, go through the phone book or go on-line and get the addresses of all the real estate offices in your area and send them each a flier advertising your business. I would advise against going into the real estate offices in person and trying to speak with anyone. They won't like this--they're too busy, so don't waste your time or take the risk of annoying a potential customer. Instead, wait to be invited before you show up at the office. Some offices may allow you to come in and briefly promote your business at their weekly office meetings. Call each office and check with the receptionist as to what their office policy may be regarding this. If you have a realtor friend, see if they can get you in to speak to their group.

HELPFUL HINT

Networking takes time. You may not see results right away. Don't get discouraged. Keep at it and it will pay off.

THE FOUR F's OF NETWORKING

1. Face-to-Face

Your potential customers need to "see" you. Let them see how talented, brilliant, and confident you are. Remember, YOU are your company's best advertisement. *Work it!*

2.   Frequency

Attend networking meetings, mixers, or events as often as you can. If your potential customers see you over and over again, they will be more likely to think of you when the time comes to hire a stager. You've got to do the work. *Show up!*

3.   Fan Out

Don't attend just one meeting. Don't be a member of just one group. Research lots of different networking clubs and/or groups and decide which ones offer the best payoff and then get out there. *Spread it around!*

4.   Follow Up

Don't forget to follow up any potential leads with a personal note or card. This is sooooo important. If you take the time to acknowledge them, they'll be more likely to hire you. *Do the "write" thing!*

I can't stress this enough:

If you want to have a successful staging business, you must keep networking.

Be a team player and join in activities with realtors. Try to identify the top producers in each real estate office, meet them, and network with them. Notice what agents or affiliates seem to be popular with everyone else and try to get to know them. Their recommendation of you will carry a lot of weight with the others. But most importantly, you must continue to network and attend those meetings even if business is booming. Never let up.

HELPFUL HINT

Check out www.mlslistings.com, and put in the name of a city in your area and do an "agent search". MLS stands for Multiple Listing Service which is a computer-based system that lets real estate agents know about properties that are for sale. Dozens of agent names are listed with all their contact information. If you study these lists, you'll see which agents are getting the most listings. Remember, we want to target the top producers.

Of my past students and the other stagers I know and work with, the ones who are consistently working and the ones who are making successes of their businesses are the ones who continue to network and promote their companies using the strategies described above. If you don't do the work, you won't *get* the work. Make the commitment and put in the time.

STAGING STORIES

Pets are a unique challenge when it comes to staging a home. It's usually best if animals can stay with friends or relatives while the house is on the market, but it's not always possible.

One story stands out in my mind.

My customer owned a pet ferret. She asked me if I was afraid of ferrets. I told her that, to be honest, I wasn't sure I actually knew what a ferret was, but I didn't think I'd be afraid. And I wasn't. The ferret was really quite sweet, but very quiet and he would sneak up on me when I wasn't looking.

I learned an interesting thing about ferrets. They can't be house-trained. They do their "business" every-where, but what's unique is that they do it in corners. As a survival instinct, they back into corners so other predators can't sneak up on them in a vulnerable moment. So I found little "piles" in corners throughout the house (even in the fireplace!).

HOMEWORK FOR CHAPTER 2

Write your 30 second infomercial. Give as much useful information as you can in those precious 30 seconds. Highlight the qualities and services that make you unique.

INFOMERCIAL:

Once you've composed your presentation, memorize it and, if possible, recite it to a friend.

Next, research clubs or networking groups in your area and try to attend at least one meeting as a guest. This will give you some experience in presenting your infomercial and help you fine tune it.

Club Name:

Date of Meeting:

Time of Meeting:

ADVERTISING

FORMS OF ADVERTISING

Word-of-mouth is a great form of advertising and best of all, it's free. Do a good job, treat your customers well, and they'll repay you by using your services again and passing your name on to others. Most other forms of advertising, however, cost money-–some of them cost a LOT of money. When you're a small business owner, and especially when you're just starting out, you may not have a lot of resources to devote to advertising and marketing. If that's the case, try to spend your advertising dollar where it will do the most good. As I've said before, you should be targeting the real estate agents in your community. By concentrating your efforts on one (or two) target groups, I believe you'll get the most return from your advertising investment, even if that investment is small.

ADVERTISING

Here are some forms of advertising you may wish to consider:

- Home improvement newspapers/magazines
- A local cable TV show devoted to real estate
- Display your business cards & other promotional materials (and a front-yard sign) at each jobsite
- Mailers, postcards, brochures, etc.
- Your own website
- Gift Certificates
- Your personal phone greeting
- Throw a party (realtors love parties)
- Sponsor lunches, seminars, or meetings realtors are likely to attend
- Hire a press agent (can be costly, but may be worth it) who can get you interviews in the TV, radio & print media
- Community meetings (churches, schools, rec centers)
- Ask others who work with real estate agents, e.g. mortgage brokers, loan agents, etc. if they can include your brochure in their own customer packages
- Write your own newsletter/blog
- Offer seminars
- Speaking engagements
- Cross-advertise with a complimentary business (painter, carpet installer, etc.)

- Magnetic signs or lettering on your car (may have some great tax benefits--ask your accountant)
- Wear a personalized T-shirt with your company info printed on the front while you're out running errands
- Occasionally change the designs on your business cards and other promotional materials to keep things fresh and unique
- Follow the lead of other successful networkers & entrepreneurs and do what they're doing

HELPFUL HINT

Be sure to keep track of testimonials you receive regarding your work. They can be used in any of your promotional materials, brochures, etc. Don't be shy about asking a customer to give you a nice referral. Most of them are happy to do it. Always ask permission from the person who gives you the testimonial before you put it in print.

As I mentioned before, the average homeowner is not going to come looking for you. Their real estate agent will. And most likely, they won't look for you in the phone book or the newspaper. They will ask other agents for referrals or call their local real estate board and they may look for a stager on-line. I would recommend at least a simple website with a few nice "before" and "after" pictures and your contact info.

Constant networking will increase the chances of getting referrals from those you network with. Just remember, one referral will lead to another and another and another. As important as it is to meet new contacts, it's equally important to stay in touch with your past customers as well. They'll be more likely to refer you if they feel you value them and their business.

PERSONAL IMAGE

The tips mentioned earlier are great advertising ideas, but of course, your very best source of advertising is YOU! Let's talk more about that.

People expect a stager to have a certain style, a certain image. If you show up at a business/marketing meeting in jeans and a T-shirt or you wear baggy sweats and sneakers to a consultation, it's doubtful your potential client will have much confidence in your ability to decorate with any skill.

Having style doesn't mean you have to wear expensive designer clothes. Think about it like this: you're going to a job interview. Dress appropriately. Dressing well is a sign of respect and conveys professionalism. Men, slacks with a clean, pressed shirt are all you need. A tie is not necessary, but no one would be offended if you wore one. Ladies, a simple skirt and sweater or nice slacks and a blouse are fine. Jazz it up in your own personal way.

Your customer *wants* you to look great. When you show up looking smart and stylish, your customer can see with their own eyes that you have great taste and design style and those are the qualities they're looking for in a stager.

HELPFUL HINT

If you can decorate the heck out of your living room, but you have trouble matching your pants to your shirt, ask a friend whose style you admire for some advice. Take her shopping with you and have her help you pick out one or two "interview" outfits. Get some inspiration from fashion or movie magazines.

And no outfit is complete without one important item-- a gorgeous, sincere smile. Remember this always--*you* are what sells your company. Be confident, be gorgeous, be you!

HOMEWORK FOR CHAPTER 3

Write an advertisement flier. Keep it simple and be
sure your message is clear from the start. Print up
some copies to take to your next networking meeting.

4

STARTING A PROJECT

THE CONSULTATION

I was a nervous wreck on my first consultation. My customer, a lovely gentleman named Harry, couldn't have been nicer and I was so blessed to work with someone so trusting and generous. He was totally open to my suggestions and ideas but he kept saying, "I don't really know much about staging." Little did he know that *I* didn't either. But I convinced him that I did and he hired me for the job. I'll never forget it because I was so excited and the job was so much fun.

For your first consultation, consider taking the following items. You will revise this list over and over again as you see what works best for you. But to get started, you may find this helpful.

- Two copies of your Check-off List (pg. 36)
- Calculator
- Contracts (pg. 46 & 47)
- Bid form (pg. 49)
- Pens
- Business cards
- Your day-planner or calendar
- Cell phone (always call when you're going to be more than five minutes late. Turn the ringer off and don't take calls during your consultation)
- Digital camera
- Portable digital recorder (great for on-the-spot "notes")
- Your GPS or a map (always keep a map in the car)
- A combination key box (pick one up at your nearest hardware store; they're about $30.00). Have this handy to put the house key into and attach to the front door or other secure location. You, your moving crew, and others may need entry into the home when the homeowner is not available to let you in.

Always have your business cards at hand. When you meet your customer at the front door, don't forget to smile and hand them one of your fabulous cards. I always remind my customers that it's O.K. to call with any questions or concerns. Always be friendly and accessible.

As you enter the house and take your first look around, even if the house is the scariest mess you've ever seen, find something (*anything*) nice to say about it. Sometimes you may be shocked at the mess, clutter, or smell, but it's always important to find something positive to say. Don't be insincere; it will be obvious. But try something like this:

"Your home has wonderful potential!"

"This wall color is perfect!"

"You're so lucky to have such spacious rooms!"

Remember that a home is very personal. Most owners are proud of their homes (even if they are a mess). Be kind and considerate of their feelings.

Many times the listing agent will be present at the consultation. Prior to the consultation, I try to speak privately with the agent to see if there are any special concerns he/she would like me to address with the customer, such as some of the things listed above (smell, clutter, etc.). Many times suggestions made by the agent are viewed as criticism by the homeowner. However, when the same suggestions come from me, the homeowner is often more willing to take the advice. Learn how to say difficult things in a kind way that won't embarrass or offend.

THE CHECK-OFF LIST

As the consultation continues, I use my check-off list as the homeowner and agent take me through the house pointing out their concerns. Once I've seen everything, I often make a few simple design suggestions. I might suggest packing away valuable and/or breakable items, removing family photos, clearing clutter, etc. These are basic staging tips (which we'll cover in Chapter 6). I may then give a more specific design recommendation such as moving the furniture in a particular way or suggesting certain accessories they may wish to add.

HELPFUL HINT

I usually bring two check-off lists--one for me and one for my client to use to keep track of the "homework" assignments I'll be giving them during our consultation. I let them make their own notes in their own way so that it makes sense to them. When doing your consultation though, be careful you don't give too much away. It would be a shame if the homeowner or their realtor took all your great design ideas and then did the work themselves. Remember, the information you have is very valuable. Don't give it away for free.

ADDRESS: _____

CLIENT: _____

PHONE: _____

CHECK-OFF LIST

Outside: Stand at curb and look at house

____ Landscaping/grass/plants_____

____ Clutter/toys/hose_____

____ Paint, color and condition_____

____ Roof_____

____ Rain Gutters_____

____ Garage Door_____

____ Front Door/hardware_____

____ Porch/doormat, porch light_____

____ Screens and Windows_____

____ Window Boxes_____

____ Shutters_____

____ Recommendations _____

Inside: Throughout house

Living Room:

____ Odors_____

____ Lighting – too dark/too bright_____

____ Paint_____

____ Carpets_____

____ Floors_____

____ Clutter_____

____ Windows_____

____ Accessories/Comments_____

_____

_____

Dining Room:

____ Odors_____

____ Lighting – too dark/too bright_____

____ Paint_____

____ Carpets_____

____ Floors_____

____ Clutter_____

____ Windows_____

____ Accessories/Comments_____

_____

_____

Kitchen:

_____ Odors_____

_____ Lighting – too dark/too bright_____

_____ Paint_____

_____ Carpets_____

_____ Floors_____

_____ Clutter_____

_____ Windows_____

_____ Accessories/Comments_____

_____

_____

Family Room:

_____ Odors_____

_____ Lighting – too dark/too bright_____

_____ Paint_____

_____ Carpets_____

_____ Floors_____

_____ Clutter_____

_____ Windows_____

_____ Accessories/Comments_____

_____

_____

Bedroom:

_____ Odors_____

_____ Lighting – too dark/too bright_____

_____ Paint_____

_____ Carpets_____

_____ Floors_____

_____ Clutter_____

_____ Windows_____

_____ Accessories/Comments_____

_____

_____

Bathroom:

_____ Odors_____

_____ Lighting – too dark/too bright_____

_____ Paint_____

_____ Carpets_____

_____ Floors_____

_____ Clutter_____

_____ Windows_____

_____ Accessories/Comments_____

_____

_____

Other:

_____ Odors_____

_____ Lighting – too dark/too bright_____

_____ Paint_____

_____ Carpets_____

_____ Floors_____

_____ Clutter_____

_____ Windows_____

_____ Accessories/Comments_____

_____

_____

Additional Recommendations:

_____

_____

_____

_____

_____

_____

_____

_____

_____

Next, I give the homeowner "homework" assignments, such as moving furniture from one room to another (or removing unneeded furniture and placing it in storage), painting, cleaning, etc. I suggest you strenuously encourage your customers to complete their assignments before you return to do the staging. If they don't, you may find *yourself* moving furniture and doing the cleaning. In that case, you may want to postpone the staging until the homeowners do their work. If they need help, and you have contractors available, hire them and don't forget to build their fees into your bid.

The next step is to take "before" pictures of all the rooms to be staged. This gives you two things; your "before" pictures for the portfolio you're preparing and a contact sheet (thumbnail-style photos all on one page) to work from as you plan your design for this project.

HELPFUL HINT

I can't tell you how many times I've gotten back to my office to prepare a design plan and find I can't remember if there was a window on a certain wall, or what color a room was painted, or how long the kitchen counters were. It's so easy to refer to your pictures.

If I've been neglectful and have forgotten my camera, I always carry a tiny, digital recorder in my purse so I can make verbal notes of those windows, paint colors, or counter lengths. Talking myself through each room helps me recall everything once I leave the property. A recorder is also a great way to make quick notes when you're driving and suddenly remember something important. Just be careful!

At this point in the consultation, I go over my checklist to make sure I haven't forgotten anything. After a while, you will most likely be able to check off all your items in your head, but when you start out it's helpful to use a list.

Be sure to have your calendar ready, so when you're asked when you can be available, you'll be prepared to answer. Try not to be rushed into a job too quickly. Make sure you have appropriate time to prepare. You want to have enough time to deliver what you've promised, which is a drop-dead, gorgeous staging job. To do less helps no one--least of all you.

However, there are times when you'll need to move fast or risk losing the job to someone who's willing and able to work within the time constraints. You do have to be flexible at times and able to think fast. Not doing so may make you less desirable than a stager who is ready to move quickly and can be counted on to jump in when help is needed.

TAKING PICTURES/YOUR PORTFOLIO

As mentioned earlier, during the consultation is the time to take your "before" pictures of each room to be staged. If you don't already have one, consider buying an inexpensive digital camera (they even have disposable ones nowadays) and learn how to use it.

Taking pictures is not as easy as it sounds. I am a terrible photographer and the pictures I take of my work are often quite unflattering. Practice, though, and you'll get better. Take pictures from all different angles, and when you're starting, take a LOT of pictures with the hopes that one or two will turn out well.

HELPFUL HINT

*You might even consider having a professional take **before** and **after** pictures for you. It's going to be more costly than doing it yourself, but if someone is using a photo to judge your work, you want to make sure it's a fantastic photo. You also may want professional shots for your brochures and other promotional materials.*

There are many great ways to display your portfolio nowadays: on a laptop, a digital frame, a video show on your website (which can be then emailed to a potential customer). If these options don't work for you, a traditional scrapbook will work just fine. Always take your portfolio with you to a job interview, or at least have a website to refer clients to. Before posting pictures on your website, it's always a good idea to get permission from the homeowner.

CONTRACTS

If the decision has been made on the spot to hire your company for the staging, have a contract ready. And by the way, congratulations.

The following examples are contracts that I designed and used for my business. Each time I had a new job, I would modify the contract to add or subtract some item. Each job teaches you something new and you want to make sure everyone's best interests are protected.

These two contracts are for two different types of jobs:

- One is a contract for staging AND furniture rental (which we'll discuss in Chapter 5).

- The other contract is for staging only.

SAMPLE CONTRACTS

You may use these contracts (pgs. 46 & 47) and modify them to suit your needs, or design a contract of your own. They are very basic and may require something more specific. You may want to consider having your lawyer help you with the wording.

HELPFUL HINT

You may feel that, in some cases, a contract is not even necessary, such as when you're working with one of your regular customers. There are certain times I don't use a contract, but remember...

If there's a dispute between you and a customer, and you don't have a contract, you also don't have a leg to stand on if you end up in court. Do what you think is best.

Contract *With* Furniture Rental

Thank you for considering XYZ STAGING COMPANY for your home staging needs. We are pleased to offer the following:

- Initial consultation $_____
- Staging fee $_____ *

      Staging fee INCLUDES home accessories rented from XYZ for up to _____ months.

* (for additional months, accessories can be rented for $_____/day and will be billed and due at end of project.

- TOTAL STAGING FEE
(excludes furniture rental fee) $_____
(staging fee due in full upon completion of staging)

- Estimated furniture rental fee
for _____ month(s) $_____
(First month's rental fee is due in full prior to staging.)
- Work can begin upon receipt of signed contract and payment.

- XYZ reserves the right to cancel this contract at any time. At such time, XYZ will be granted immediate entry to the property to remove all items belonging to XYZ.

- PROJECT NOT TO EXCEED $_____

Miscellaneous:

_____

_____

We agree to all the terms and costs listed above:

Client: _____   Date: _____

Stager: _____   Date: _____

46

Contract *Without* Furniture Rental

Thank you for considering XYZ STAGING COMPANY for your
home staging needs. We are pleased to offer the following:

- Initial consultation $_____
- Staging fee $_____ *

    Staging fee INCLUDES home accessories rented from
    XYZ for up to _____ months.

*(for additional months, accessories can be rented for $_____/day
and will be billed and due at end of project.)

- TOTAL STAGING FEE $_____
  (staging fee due in full upon completion of staging)

- Work can begin upon receipt of signed contract.

- XYZ reserves the right to cancel this contract at any time. At such
  time, XYZ will be granted immediate entry to the property to remove all items belonging to XYZ.

Miscellaneous:

_____

_____

We agree to all the terms and conditions listed above:

Client: _____ Date: _____

Stager: _____ Date: _____

I have the person who is going to be responsible for paying me sign as the "client" whether it is the home-owner or the agent. If the customer has not signed the contract at the time of our consultation, I will fax the completed contract to the client, have them sign it, and fax it back.

HELPFUL HINT

Any handwritten changes to the contract should be made above the signatures and then initialed by all parties.

SAMPLE BID

Sometimes I use my contract as both the bid and the contract. It saves time to do it that way, but once in a while the sight of a contract can make a potential client feel pressured. If I have any concerns about scaring off a customer, I will submit a friendly-looking bid for his/her approval and once approval is obtained, I will fax over that scary contract.

The following is a sample bid. But keep in mind that how you write your bid will depend on how you price your jobs. It will also depend on how much you want to reveal to your customer about how you determine the price of your work. I would be cautious about re-vealing too much. We'll talk more about pricing later.

XYZ STAGING COMPANY BID FORM

Initial Consultation $_____

Staging fee $_____

Accessories rental
for _____ month(s) $_____

Pick up & delivery $_____

TOTAL STAGING PROJECT
NOT TO EXCEED $_____

THANK YOU NOTES

Once the consultation is complete, and you're ready to leave, be sure to smile, thank everyone for their time, then head back to your office and write your thank you notes. Here are some samples if you need help.

Dear (homeowners):

Thank you both so much for the opportunity to meet with you and present a staging bid for your beautiful home. I appreciate your consideration and I am looking forward to working with you on this exciting project. Since we covered a lot of material today, don't hesitate to contact me if you have any further questions or concerns.

Again, thank you and best wishes for a quick and profitable sale!

Sincerely,

Dear (agent):

Thank you so much for the opportunity to present a staging bid for your beautiful listing at 123 Maple St. The house is wonderful with lots of potential and great features. I already have some exciting staging strategies planned to make it even more special.

Whatever you decide, I thank you for your consideration and wish you all the best for a quick and profitable sale!

Sincerely,

Notice that all references to the house are kept positive. Don't use fake flattery. Be as sincere as you can. A simple, nicely worded note holds a lot of value.

STAGING STORIES

Clutter is, in my opinion, *the* biggest turn off and yet the easiest and cheapest problem to fix.

I have seen some of the most amazing, jaw-dropping clutter you can imagine.

At one house, I couldn't tell you what color the carpet was—I really couldn't swear there *was* carpet. And I didn't see one inch of countertop anywhere.

Another customer had paper bags full of bath towels in her fireplace and newspapers piled inside her stove.

Once you help a customer eliminate all the unnecessary clutter in their homes, it will change their lives.

It's the number-one homework assignment I give my clients.

HOMEWORK FOR CHAPTER 4

Using the check-off list (pg. 36), go around your own home, or the house of a friend and make design notes and recommendations. Look at the home with a "stager's eye."

JOB TYPES

JOB TYPES

Once you've done your consultation, made your notes, taken your pictures, and given the homeowners their homework assignments, it's time to go back to the office and plan your design strategy. Here's how I break down the different job types.

Homeowner-Occupied During the Staging

Many owners will continue to live in their homes during the time their house is on the market. If their furniture and accessories are in good shape, you may just need to do some "redesigning" to make better use of what they already have. My experience, however, is that most homeowners need some help. Usually a few pieces of artwork may be needed, or a lamp, or some plants. It surprises me how many people do not have *one* set of bath towels that match. Maybe the kitchen needs a throw rug, or maybe the dining table could use a couple of elegant place settings. Sometimes (though rarely), I never need to bring anything extra to the job. I do a redesign using the homeowner's belongings and nothing from my own inventory.

HELPFUL HINT

Doing homeowner "redesigns" without adding any accessories of your own may be a good way to begin your staging career and there are certainly pluses to this type of strategy, e.g. no money or inventory needed to get started, no packing, no storage needed, etc.

This bedroom was staged using only things the home-owner already had in the house. **Nothing new was added**. Now this once-ordinary bedroom really has some style.

Below is an example of how I **added to the home-owner's belongings** with accessories from my staging inventory.

Empty/Vacant Property

Using Furniture and Accessories

Think back to the last time you were in a model home. Wasn't it pretty with all the fancy furniture and designer accessories? Now, how do you think you would've liked that same property if it was empty? It probably wouldn't have appealed to you in the same way it did when it was furnished. Staging can help create that same appeal in your client's home.

If a property is vacant, I strongly recommend that my customer furnish the property, at least two or three rooms. Now you're thinking-- where am I going to get enough furniture to furnish two or three rooms? Simple. You rent it. Go to your phonebook or the Internet and find the nearest furniture rental company in your area. We'll talk more about this in a minute.

HELPFUL HINT

In a vacant house, I recommend furnishing and accessorizing usually the living room, dining room, kitchen and the bathrooms. If the budget allows, I'd also furnish the master bedroom.

Accessorizing Only (Vignettes)

Furniture rental can get expensive, and in some cases, your client may not be willing or able to afford it. In that case, see if your customer would agree to "accessorizing" only (or creating vignettes to give the illusion of furniture). This has been, in my experience, a very successful and affordable solution. Accessorize what you can, e.g. the kitchen counters, bathrooms, built-in bookcases, shelves, desks. A picture over the mantle, some candlesticks on the hearth, and a "picnic" in front of the fireplace adds warmth and energy to the house and makes a much better impression than a cold, vacant property.

Below is an example of **accessorizing only** (or creating a "vignette") in a home with no furniture.

RENTING FURNITURE

As I mentioned before, you'll want to check out the furniture rental companies in your area. The prices, styles, and quality will vary from store to store. Drop in or make an appointment to visit the showroom staff and meet who'll be helping you with your staging orders.

HELPFUL HINT

I suggest developing a rapport with the showroom staff. They will be more willing to answer the many questions you'll have as you get started. Also, many of them give dead-on design advice, and because they know their inventory intimately, I find their input incredibly valuable.

Look around at their inventory and see how they've got furniture grouped and arranged. See what items you really like. Think about how those pieces will fit with the accessories you have. You may want to do this BEFORE you buy any accessories, so that you can coordinate your accessories with the rental furniture. You can work with one rental company or several companies. Check out each company's staging policies, procedures, and pricing (there may be minimum rental fees which can make your job challenging, so find out).

You'll get to know the inventory frontwards and back-
wards before too long, but until then, you may need to
go into the showroom each time you have a job to look
at the pieces again, mix and match things and check
prices. Soon, you'll know the name of each couch,
chair, lamp or picture, the cost of each item and what
other items they'll coordinate with in the inventory.
Then it will be easy to place an order over the phone.
Since you may need to visit the showroom frequently
as you get started, it might be a good idea to work with
a rental company that's close to your home or office.

When I'm selecting furniture for a particular project, I
take a number of things into consideration—the first
being the cost of each piece of furniture. If choosing
between two similar couches, I will usually opt for the
least expensive. I also want to stage appropriately for
the style of the house, the type of neighborhood, and
the potential buyers. Zebra-print pillows and bear-skin
rugs have their place. But usually not in the houses *I*
stage.

Most of your customers are going to be thrilled with
whatever furniture and accessories you select. It's a
chance for them to have a professional decorator come
into their home and design something spectacular
(usually at their agent's expense) and they love it.

But of course, you can't please everyone. Try not to
take it personally if your customer is not happy with
the results of your staging. If your client is unhappy,

it's usually because the décor you've selected does not reflect their personal taste.

HELPFUL HINT

Of course the goal of properly staging a home for sale is to make it appeal to as many people as possible. However, some homeowners will want you to decorate according to their own personal tastes. You'll have to gently explain how it's to their advantage that you design for the buying public, not a specific individual. This customer may be a good candidate for future business. Offer to help her design her <u>new</u> home exactly the way she'd like it.

Below is an example of a dramatic change with some clean up and **rental furniture**.

Here's another example of **vacant** vs. **rental furniture**. There's no denying the attraction to the furnished room.

FURNITURE RENTAL COMPANIES

There are only a few decent furniture rental companies in my area. You'll need to research what's available in your area. Different companies offer different services, styles, selections, prices, and quality. Some companies may be good for certain jobs but not for others. You'll get to know what they each offer as you gain some experience. I found a company that I preferred to work with regularly because I could always depend on them for service and quality. You'll find your favorite too.

When you find out what companies are available in your area, stop by and visit each one. Notice how the staff behaves with customers and walk-ins. Check out the furniture styles and selection. Ask some questions, pick up brochures, and be sure to find out what the process is for renting furniture for a staging project. Stagers are sometimes required to rent for longer periods than the average citizen and there may be other requirements that are specific to stagers.

STAGING STORIES

When a customer refuses to make some of the changes you've suggested, you'll just have to deal with it, or consider walking away from the job.

One sweet, little old lady refused to remove the 80-odd pictures of Jesus and the dozens of little angels and Mother Mary figurines from her home. I had to respect that. It was, after all, her home.

There will be some customers who just won't let you do your job. Sometimes, you may want to consider walking away.

When a customer says "nobody's coming over to look at my stuff, they're coming to look at the house," I know it's hopeless. That customer will not cooperate and there won't be much I can do to help. The truth is, people DO look at their "stuff" and if there's a lot of it, potential buyers will be distracted or turned off. These stubborn homeowners are fooling themselves if they think otherwise.

I ask if I can at least "rearrange" the pictures or fig-urines. If the answer is yes, I put them in less con-spicuous places or cluster them in one general area so they're not spread all over the house.

PRICING YOUR WORK

Staging stands to earn your customer a nice return on their investment and you should consider that when pricing your jobs.

Stagers can charge anywhere from $500.00 to $5,000.00 or more per job. That's why staging can be such a lucrative full or part-time job.

The fee you charge depends on what your homeowners, their neighborhood, and the market will support, and what particular staging services you provide. If you chose to do more large high-end homes, you'll be able to charge higher fees. But there will also be more labor involved per job, you'll need a larger inventory, more storage, etc. and thus you'll have a higher cost of doing business.

If your niche is staging the "average home," your fees will need to be reasonable for the average homeowner.

If you chose not to have your own inventory of accessories, but use the homeowner's belongings instead, then of course your business costs will be much lower and you'll only need to charge for your time.

There are many factors to consider when deciding what you'll charge for a job. Here are some thoughts on how you might determine your fee (your net profit):

- Base your fee on estimated hours and accessories rental (furniture rental is separate)

- Base your fee on the square footage of the house being sold

- Base your fee on the number of rooms to be staged

- Base your fee on a percentage of the sales price

Other considerations

- Will you charge for your consultations? (some stagers do free consultations, others charge a fee, others charge a fee and then deduct it from the cost of the job if they're hired)
- How many accessories you're devoting to the job (what rental fee will you charge your customer for the use of your accessories?)
- How long can your customer rent your accessories for that fee?
- How many hours will the job take, from beginning to end?
  - Include time for coordinating the project & any administrative duties
  - Include time spent packing all the accessories you'll be using

- ▪ Actual time spent at the property doing the staging (add extra time if homeowner or other visitors are going to be present—see the Staging Story on page 100)
- ▪ Time spent de-staging once the job is over
- How much travel time and mileage is involved?
- Phone calls, faxes and emails
- Insurance
- Advertising
- Damage protection (some of your accessories will get broken, stolen, or lost. Some of them will start looking tired and worn and you'll need to replace them.)
- Storage facility fees for your inventory
- Assistant stagers or other staff

See if you can find out what other stagers in your area are charging. You want to be competitive, but also be careful that you're not doing the work too cheaply. There can be a wide range of pricing from stager to stager but I try not to get hung up on what others are charging. I determine for myself what I want to get paid for the time and effort I put into a job.

It may take some practice and experience to perfect your pricing strategy. Pricing a job just right is chal-lenging. You'll get the hang of it, though. Be patient.

HELPFUL HINT

Keep close track of all your time and expenses as you're getting started so you can begin to see what your true costs are. It will aid you in determining the price of your jobs. It's important to be paid for all the work you do and all the expenses you incur in the course of a job.

OFFICE WORKSHEETS

Though now I can usually calculate a bid in my head, when I started, I'd come back to the office after my consultation and write everything out on a worksheet to help me remember all the things I wanted to consider. Once I was sure I had everything just right, I would present the bid to my customer.

I'd suggest using this strategy as you're getting started. You don't want to blurt out a bid on the spot. I can just about guarantee you you'll either over bid and lose the job or under bid and be stuck doing more work than what you're being paid for.

See if the worksheets on the following pages help you. On the first sample, I've included a column for "hours" as well as "$" so you can start to see how much time you're spending on each project. Are you getting paid for all that time? Worksheets 2 and 3 offer different strategies for pricing your work.

OFFICE WORKSHEET (1)

STAGING:	Hours	Fee
Consultation	_____	$_____
Prep time	_____	$_____
Travel	_____	$_____
Labor (time spent at the property)	_____	$_____
Administrative (time & administrative costs associated with project, e.g. phone calls, faxes, correspondence)	_____	$_____
De-staging at job completion	_____	$_____
TOTAL Hours & Staging Fee	_____	$_____

(Staging fee does <u>not</u> include furniture or accessories, see below)

Discounts (if any)   (-) _____ $_____

NEW TOTAL $_____

Accessories Rental for _____ months $_____

Furniture Rental for _____ months $_____

**TOTAL _____ MONTH PROJECT
NOT TO EXCEED** $_____

OFFICE WORKSHEET (2)

<u>NUMBER OF ROOMS:</u> ($_____ per room)

Living Room	__X__	$_____
Dining Room	_____	$_____
Kitchen	_____	$_____
Family Room	_____	$_____
Bedroom #_____	_____	$_____
Master Bedroom	_____	$_____
Master Bathroom	_____	$_____
Bathroom #_____	_____	$_____
Misc.	_____	$_____
	TOTAL	$_____
Furniture Rental		$_____
	TOTAL	$_____

OFFICE WORKSHEET (3)

Calculating an Hourly Rate

How much money do you
want to make per year: $_____

Divide that amount by
52 (weeks): $_____

Divide that amount by the
# of hours per job: $_____

This is your hourly rate: $_____

HELPFUL HINT

Remember, the worksheet is for your eyes only. You do not need to share it with your customer.

BILLING YOUR CUSTOMER

Personally, I request payment for my staging services on the day of the job. Once my services have been performed, I like to receive payment. Being paid the day of the job also creates less office work for me. If I can collect a check right at the jobsite, I don't have to send out invoices, make phone calls, or hunt people down to collect my pay.

HELPFUL HINT

For approximately $30.00 per month, and a small per-transaction amount, you can set up an on-line system to accept credit cards. Look for an option that has a "virtual terminal." It's very simple to use and you don't have to have a piece of equipment to lug around. Accepting credit cards may make you more attractive to certain clients whose cash budgets may be tight.

Sometimes I have to be flexible and wait for payment somewhere down the road. That's O.K. with me most of the time. You'll need to decide if it's O.K. with you.

Billing suggestions may include:

- payment due on the day of the job (as mentioned above),
- invoicing the customer on the 30th of the month, payment due on the 15th of the following month, or something similar, or
- payment received out of escrow.

I have a lot of requests to be paid out of escrow. Escrow is an arrangement where money or documents are held in trust by a third party until certain agreed-upon conditions are met.

Though many stagers are willing to accept payment through escrow, I'm not crazy about the idea. If the home is taken off the market for some reason, then there will be *no escrow*. If I agree to this arrangement, I ALWAYS do a contract stating that *"Parties agree that payment will be made through escrow. If the house is taken off the market for ANY reason, or any other changes are made to the original contract, the staging fee becomes due in full immediately."*

Again, having your lawyer look over the wording may be a good idea.

HOMEWORK FOR CHAPTER 5

Visit several furniture rental companies in your area. Start taking stock of their inventory. Introduce yourself as a new stager and ask them to explain how you would go about renting furniture for a staging project. Pick up any brochures and see if they have a website showing their furniture inventory so you can study it from the comfort of your own home.

Company #1 (address & phone number):

_____

Contact name: _____

Company #2 (address & phone number):

_____

Contact name: _____

STAGING & OTHER SERVICES

STAGING BASICS

Let's go over some basic staging concepts. Whether the home you're staging is a high-end property or your average tract home, townhouse, or condo, these staging tips will work equally well for all. Not all jobs involve glamorous designer furniture or one-of-a-kind artwork and accessories. Either way, it doesn't really matter. You approach each job the same. And these tips will help you get started.

You will learn more about design and decorating as you get more experience, but the following will give you the basics of staging. These items are some of the "homework" assignments I give my customers.

STAGE IT WELL, WATCH IT SELL!®

Personal Photos/Items

Remove all family photos, baby/pet pictures, etc.
Remove any other personal items like trophies,
diplomas, awards, and refrigerator art. These
items "personalize" the space and often distract
buyers from what's important. It also makes it
more difficult for the buyers to imagine themselves living there.

Religious/Cultural Artwork and Icons

This is a little touchy and some of your customers may not appreciate the suggestion to pack
away their religious items and decorations. Be
sensitive to their feelings and kindly explain how
important it is that their house appeals to buyers
from all walks of life, cultures, and spiritual
beliefs.

Collectibles

Many of us have collections of some kind or
another--lighthouses, angels, coffee mugs, etc.
In most cases, I'd eliminate any collections and
ask the customer to pack them away. Depending
on the type of collection (and if my own selection of accessories is low), I may decide to use
their collectibles in the staging. As we discussed

before, gather them from around the house and display them in one area.

Wild Colors on the Walls

If rooms or certain walls have been painted in bright or wild accent colors, I'll usually suggest a quick paint job. In general, aim for "neutral" when staging. Again, we want this home to appeal to the widest audience possible. Bright, bold colors may turn off a lot of people. Neutral doesn't necessarily mean "white," however. In past years, stagers used to suggest nothing but "real estate beige." But the current trend is to bring back color--even for staging jobs. Sage greens, buttery yellows and warm tans will work well with most decors, and if used correctly, darker, more dramatic colors can add some elegance.

If your homeowners can't or won't paint their purple and orange walls, you'll just have to work with them. I find that black and white artwork fits well when there are lots of competing colors. Be careful when adding more color and busy patterns and designs to rooms with brightly-colored walls.

Clean, Clean, Clean

There may be many detractors in the home you're staging, but a lot can be forgiven if the house is sparkling clean. Again, this can be a touchy subject. It's often awkward and uncomfortable to tell someone that they need to clean their home, but it's in their best interest. I usually say something like, "Your cleaning crew needs to be scheduled prior to the staging." Even if they don't have a cleaning crew, it's a graceful way to send the message that cleaning must be done.

It's a good idea to establish your own network of handymen, cleaning crews, painters, carpet installers, etc. That way, you can be a full-service company. Homeowners have enough to do when it comes to selling their homes. They're going to be overwhelmed and any help you can give them will make you a very desirable person to work with.

And referring these contractors may result in other business opportunities for you since they will be more likely to reciprocate by recommending you to a prospective client. You never know where your next job may come from.

Aaaah…from cluttered to calm. **Eliminate clutter** and keep it simple.

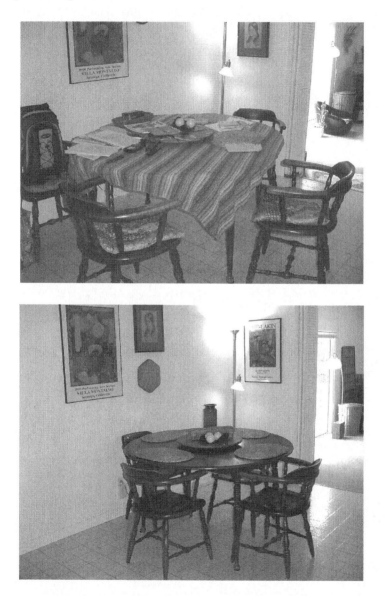

Less Is More

My own staging philosophy is to keep it simple and uncluttered. I don't believe the home has to be stuffed with furniture and accessories to be beautiful and make a powerful statement. My suggestion to you would be to try to resist adding *too much*. Keep it simple. The correct amount of staging will properly camouflage the negative aspects of the property and perfectly highlight the positive features of the home.

Furniture Layout

I was never one to use a tape measure or draw out floor plans when designing a room layout for one of my projects. If the room was empty and I was going to be furnishing it, I would just "eye-ball" it. Not everyone is good at this, however. You may want to start out at least doing some simple measurements and a rough sketch of the room layout to help you with your design, but drawing complicated floor plans is not necessary.

When arranging, be sure to keep furniture from blocking the flow of traffic, doorways, windows, sliding doors, etc. You may need to be creative. I love to put furniture at an angle--it really makes a room interesting. A couch at an angle by the fireplace or a bed in the corner of the bedroom will also sometimes open up an over-crowded room arrangement.

I don't like to walk into a room and see the back of a couch or chair. It presents not only a physical barrier, but sometimes it may cause an emotional barrier as well. Try to place furniture in a way that leaves the entry into the room open and spacious. When the rooms are small to begin with, a feeling of spaciousness will be especially important.

Even though I like placing furniture at angles, you'll see in the following photos how the couch angled in the entryway blocks off the room and makes it look overcrowded. This arrangement is fine for everyday living, but it's a no-no for staging.

Below is an example of **furniture layout** that keeps the room open and spacious and eliminates barriers. Clearing excess clutter also helps to create a more spacious and inviting room.

When I started staging, I did a lot of experimenting with furniture arrangement. I was often able to come up with simple solutions to design problems that my clients had struggled with and hated about their homes for years. Your understanding of design principles will evolve as you gain more experience.

HELPFUL HINT

Go to your local home goods store (such as Linens n' Things) and buy some "furniture moving sliders," which are plastic disks that fit under the feet of heavy couches, chairs, tables, etc.

Using them, you can easily slide a heavy piece of furniture from one place to another. They're great and have saved my back hundreds of times. They cost about $10 and you'll love them. You can find them on-line too.

We are so lucky to have an unlimited, non-ending supply of information right at our fingertips, any time of the day or night. I'm talking, of course, about the Internet. I am forever scouring the Internet for information on design, staging, and decorating. I like to see what other stagers from all across the country (and even in other countries) are doing and I want to make sure I keep current on trends in design. I suggest you do the same, especially if, like me, you are a self-taught decorator.

OTHER SERVICES YOUR COMPANY MAY OFFER

Many of your clients are going to be so impressed with the decorating you did for their staging project, that they may ask you to come to their new home and help them decorate there. What a compliment! Think about how and what you may want to charge for this service. See the chapter on Pricing Your Work (review Chapter 5).

I get requests to assist with:

- selecting paint, tile, or carpet
- selecting furniture and accessories
- redesigning a room/rooms
- personal shopping
- decorating for parties, holidays, & special events

I also get requests to help with "remodels," which may mean tearing down walls, moving plumbing, recon-figuring tub and toilet placement, or relocating kitchen sinks and dishwashers. Since I'm not trained for such a project, it would be inappropriate for me to accept this type of work.

HELPFUL HINT

Remodeling is NOT a service I provide, since I have no experience in designing floor plans or tearing down walls. I'd strongly advise you to stay away from projects that are beyond the scope of your knowledge, talents, and training.

GIFT CERTIFICATES

I find gift certificates to be a fun, easy way to earn a few extra dollars. Usually a real estate agent purchases a gift certificate from me for an hour of design time, and gives it to a customer as a thank you gift. Others have given them to that person on their list who "has everything." Others still give it to friends or family who may enjoy the experience of a quick room redesign, or someone who may be thinking of selling their home and needs help with staging.

You may wish to donate a gift certificate to be auctioned off at a fundraiser for a local school or other community organization. Gift certificates are also great advertising gimmicks or giveaways for the realtor marketing meetings you attend.

HOMEWORK FOR CHAPTER 6

Visit your local paint store and see if you can pick up a
"paint fan." You are going to be asked quite often to
suggest paint colors for your staging customers. I keep
my paint fan in my car at all times. If you're unsure
about what colors to suggest, try talking with other
stagers and see what they recommend. Not all stagers
are going to want to share information with you, but
some will. Go to lots of open houses and study the
work of other stagers. If you see a wall color you like,
don't be shy about pulling out your paint fan and trying
to match the color. The realtor you work with may also
be able to suggest some great color options.

Color name, brand, #: _____

Color name, brand, #: _____

Color name, brand, #: _____

Color name, brand, #: _____

7

PURCHASING ACCESSORIES & FURNITURE

PURCHASING YOUR OWN ACCESSORIES

It's impossible for me to say how much you should spend on accessories as you're getting started. The thing I love about this business is that you can start with virtually nothing. If you don't have much of a budget, only accept the jobs you can stage using things you already own. If you have some money to invest in an inventory, go for it. You can spend as much or as little as you wish. I can go crazy buying accessories; it's one of my favorite things to do. But initially, I didn't have much, and when I could, I added more.

HELPFUL HINT

Add to your inventory as you gain experience as a stager. Knowing more about staging and design will help you make smarter purchases so you can get the most value out of your staging budget.

As we discussed before, some jobs won't require any additional accessories, but in my experience, most jobs do. When I shop for accessories, I look for items that are inexpensive, a good size (little knick-knacks don't make much impact), non-breakable, neutral, with lots of style. I get most of my accessories at Marshalls, Ross, Target, Walmart, and TJ Maxx. Their prices are great and they always have lots of interesting bits and pieces. My favorites include:

Marshalls	Pictures Table top decorations (excellent prices and styles) Decorative oil and vinegar bottles with bright colors that are great for spicing up the kitchen.
Ross	See above
Target	Table top decorations Bath towels and accessories Bath rugs Lamps

Walmart   Silk plants (great prices)
Comforter sets, bed pillows
Affordable area rugs
Bath towels and accessories
Bath rugs
Kitchen dish towels
Kitchen throw rugs
Throw pillows
Candles
Fake fruit, bread (they have a Styro-
foam croissant that looks so real the
last one I used in a staging job came
back with teeth marks in it)

TJ Maxx   Pictures (my favorite place to shop
for artwork)
Table top decorations

Some staging jobs may require accessories of a more
expensive and/or elegant nature and of course there are
countless stores or boutiques that can help you out.

Your local furniture consignment store often has a
wonderful variety of unusual furniture pieces and
accessories. If I have a customer who's looking for
something unique, I can often find just the right thing at
my favorite consignment store.

I get lots of things from people who are cleaning out
their homes and want to get rid of stuff. I go to garage
sales and flea markets too. Accessories can be found

anywhere. The neighborhood dollar store can hold many treasures. When I need dinner plates, for example, I get them for a buck apiece. They're fantastic and I love the great colors and patterns. Besides, when a plate gets broken, it's a lot less painful if you only paid a dollar for it.

HELPFUL HINT

I have some accessories that are dated and more old-fashioned. But I keep them, because sometimes I need such items. If I'm staging "grandma's house" and she has hand-made doilies everywhere and a crocheted toilet paper cover, this is where those more dated items will fit right in, so don't throw them out. Somewhere, someday, you'll need them.

If you don't have a big budget to buy lots of accessories, you might need to get creative. For example, when I started, I bought some inexpensive bath towel sets. I'd then take the hand towel, roll it up, and tie a bunch of raffia or a pretty ribbon around it. I'd place it on the bathroom counter with some pretty soaps in a little dish. You see, I made an *extra* accessory out of the hand towel I already had. A cake stand looks cute in the bathroom with little soaps stacked up on top. Different-sized candles on top of a cake stand will also make an interesting accessory in the bathroom, or any-where.

Go to the dollar store and buy some colorful kitchen towels. Roll them and place them in a basket and put it on the kitchen counter next to the sink. Or use a collection of your customer's odd bath towels rolled and stacked in a pyramid on the side of the tub.

Most of us own a collection of odd, cheap, glass vases. Gather them together and spray paint them all white (or a color to match your homeowner's décor). You now have a dramatic gallery of glasswork to display on the shelves.

Here's an idea I love; soak the label off a full bottle of wine. Next, take a gold-paint pen and write out a dinner menu on the side of the bottle. Place it in the center of a table you've set using your cute dishes from the dollar store.

A friend of mine had an inspired idea--she took one large, inexpensive print (you could use a poster, a picture from a calendar, etc.) and cut it into four pieces. Then she framed each piece separately and hung them together in an eye-catching display. For the price of one print and four inexpensive frames, you have a wonderful, coordinated gallery of artwork.

Even wrapping paper or fabric can be framed and used as artwork.

See what I mean? Maybe these particular ideas don't suit your taste or style, but my point is…be creative. You don't need to spend a lot of money. Heck, when I started, I was pulling pictures, candlestick holders, wine glasses, and dinner plates out of my own home.

If you're low on accessories, don't be shy about "shopping" through your customer's belongings. Colorful ceramic dishes and salad bowls look beautiful filled with fruit or floating candles. A grouping of *empty* picture frames can make a dramatic display on a bare wall. A collection of odd water pitchers, brass candlestick holders, or birdhouses will charm anyone. A large arrangement of old record albums (not the cover, but the disks) looks amazing on the wall over a black leather couch or on display in a media room. The list goes on and on.

HELPFUL HINT

Scour magazines and look carefully in the background of your favorite TV shows for design ideas and inspiration. HGTV has tons of info and helpful ideas. Go through model homes, go to open houses and see what your competition is doing. Inspiration is all around you.

BUYING YOUR OWN FURNITURE

Stagers who are ready to commit to a full-time staging career will need to consider purchasing their own furniture at some point. If this is just a part-time job for you however, I wouldn't necessarily recommend this route. It will be a huge commitment and these are some things to consider:

- storing or warehousing the furniture
- cleaning the furniture
- updating the furniture & keeping current with trends
- replacing damaged/out-of-style pieces
- rental on the storage/warehouse facility
- hiring a moving crew to pack, deliver, and pick up furniture for each job
- payroll/benefits, etc. for employees (moving men/women, assistant stagers and other staff)
- purchasing/renting a truck to make deliveries and pick ups

Not all stagers will choose this path, though it may certainly have its benefits. For example, *you* get to decide what to charge for furniture rental, instead of being at the mercy of a rental company. By doing so, it can make you more competitive and you can likely under-bid your competition. But the flip side is the extra work involved (as mentioned above). It wasn't the right career move for me, but it may be for you. You

can tailor your staging career to suit your own needs
and desires.

If you're going to purchase furniture, check with your
local furniture rental company. They might, as mine
does, have a clearance center where they sell the gently
used or older pieces for great prices. For example, they
may have a perfectly fine couch or chair, but it might
have a rip on the back. They can't use it anymore because they won't know how the item may be placed in
the home, but you can use it, knowing that you can
place the damaged side up against a wall.

Again, start scouring your neighborhood garage sales
for low-priced treasures. Check the flea market, the
thrift store, consignment stores, discount furniture
stores and warehouses and take any hand-me-downs
you can get. Be creative--it's what you do best!

You can start small, but to do any real volume of work,
you'll need a larger inventory at some point, as well as
a place to store it.

HELPFUL HINT

*Though I don't keep a furniture inventory, I quite often
have a need for just one small piece of furniture to
complete a job, e.g. a bistro set (little table with two*

(Continued)

chairs) for the kitchen or dining nook, or a coffee and/or end table. It's not often feasible to rent just one piece of furniture due to the cost involved. To solve the problem, I purchased a small, inexpensive round table (the legs unscrew for easy transport) and covered it with a tablecloth. I bought two little chairs at a second-hand store, painted them myself and recovered their seats to match the tablecloth. Now I have a "bistro" set when I need it, and it cost me next to nothing.

STORING YOUR ACCESSORIES

When you build up an inventory of accessories, you're going to need somewhere to store them. I'm very fortunate that I have storage available in my home. It saves me the cost of storage rental fees, but what's better is that I have access to my inventory at any time, day or night.

If I need to prepare and pack for a job at midnight, that's O.K., because I'm in the safety of my own home. I wouldn't want to be at the storage facility by myself at midnight.

When you're first starting out, try storing your accessories at home or in the garage. If that's not possible, you may need to find a storage facility near your home or office. It may be expensive and if you have a large inventory you're really going to need some space. Check around for pricing, security, and a convenient location.

HAULING YOUR ACCESSORIES

I have a car with lots of cargo space, which is helpful in this business. If your car has no cargo space, you may want to consider (at some point) buying an inexpensive truck or car that you can use for the purpose of hauling your accessories to and from your jobsites. Or maybe you can borrow a friend's car or rent a car or small truck when necessary. You might even consider hiring one of the neighbor's kids to do pickups and deliveries using *their* truck. Just be sure to build this fee into your bid.

If you have no cargo space and are unable to pack a lot of items in the car you do have, perhaps you should start your business doing redesigns only. It may limit the type of work you'll be able to do, but it's an excellent option.

PACKING YOUR ACCESSORIES FOR A JOB

When I started, I used plain, old cardboard boxes to pack my accessories in when I had a job. I soon discovered that boxes are too bulky, odd shaped, they usually don't have handles to grab onto, the bottoms fall out with a heavy load, and they wear out quickly.

Instead of using boxes, go to your favorite hardware store and buy some plastic bins. Make sure they "nest" (one fits inside another). You can find good ones with matching lids for about $5. Don't get one that's too big, because when it's fully packed, you won't be able to lift it. I like these bins because they have sturdy handles with smooth edges, you can cram a lot of stuff in them, they're washable, re-useable, and they're easy to store when not in use.

UNPACKING AFTER A JOB

When the house you've staged is sold and your job is over, you'll need to pick up all your accessories and bring them back to store until the next time you use them. Take them to your storage space and unpack immediately.

HELPFUL HINT

Put everything back in its proper place, wash anything that needs cleaning (rugs, towels, glassware, etc.), throw out anything damaged and stack your bins for the next time. When the next job pops up, you'll be ready to roll.

STAGING STORIES

Kids. Sweet as they are, it's hard to work when they're underfoot.

I'll never forget little Kaitlin, who followed me everywhere I went. Touched everything I put down. Moved everything I placed. Undid everything I put together. And said nothing but "Oh my. Oh my. Oh my." over and over and over again. I can laugh now, because she was so cute and funny. But at the time, I wasn't sure I'd ever get done with my work. Oh my.

If I have my way, I prefer no one be at home when I'm there to do the staging. No matter how unobtrusive the homeowner tries to be during the time I'm there working, having someone there always creates a delay (I don't get paid for delays). If I know the homeowners plan on being present on the staging day, I will do one of two things:

1. Charge extra (must be done on the original bid).

2. Offer them a "Meal and a Matinee." As above, I build an extra $50.00 into my original fee. On the day of the staging, I give the homeowners the $50.00 to go out for a few hours for lunch and a movie. They love it and I then have the house to myself to do my work uninterrupted.

HOMEWORK FOR CHAPTER 7

If your budget permits, go to your local hardware store and purchase a few packing bins. Look for ones with soft, rounded edges and removable lids. You might not use the lids, but keep them just in case. The bins that have lids that are permanently attached will just get in your way. They also tend to break easily and the broken edges can be very sharp and dangerous.

Next, check out one of the stores recommended in this chapter and begin checking out possible inventory selections. Try to find accessories that will work well together, rather than odd, random pieces. As you start building your inventory, don't buy something just because you like it, but because it will work well with other accessories you already own. Also check around your own home for things you're not using anymore that you may be able to use in your first few staging jobs.

OFFICE / PAPERWORK

BOOKKEEPING/INVOICING/RECORDS

These days, there are countless computer programs that can help you keep track of your records and manage your bookkeeping. And of course, there's nothing wrong with consulting a professional. I'm not very computer-savvy, so I do things the old-fashioned way.

I use the following (easily found at any office store):

- An accordion file, divided with a tab for each month,
- a hard-bound record-keeping book,
- two file folders, and
- an inexpensive calendar or day planner.

When I have a receipt for a business purchase (accessories, postage, client lunch receipt, stationery, thank you gifts, printer ink, etc.), I circle the date and the total on the receipt. Then I log each receipt in the hard-bound book. I label each page in the book as follows:

Date	Description	Receipt Y/N	Expense	Income

After I log the receipt amount under "Expense," I put the receipt in the accordion file folder under the appropriate month. At the end of the month, I total up all the expenses and all the income (more about that below) for that month. At the end of the year, all I do is add up the totals for expenses and income to use when filing my income taxes.

Next, I label my two file folders:

1. Invoices Outstanding + the year
2. Invoices Paid + the year

When I invoice a customer, I make a copy for him/her and a copy for me. Their copy goes to them, of course, and my copy goes in my Invoices Outstanding file. When I receive their check, I fill in the amount paid and the date received and then I file it in the Invoices Paid folder. Remember to put the month's received invoices total in your hard-bound book under the "Income" heading.

HELPFUL HINT

I make my own invoices on the computer so I never run out, I can redesign them whenever I wish, and I can easily email them to my customers when needed. There are also countless free invoice templates online that you can use. They're super professional and you can personalize them with clipart, testimonials, etc. Don't forget to turn them into PDF files if you're going to email them to your customer.

SAMPLE INVOICE

Have a look at the following invoice sample. I use it as my customer's receipt as well because I'm always trying to minimize my office and paperwork.

You are welcome to use this design as your own or use it as inspiration to create an invoice that suits your needs.

ADDRESS: _____

CLIENT NAME/PHONE: _____

INVOICE/RECEIPT

XYZ STAGING COMPANY

Your business is greatly appreciated.

THANK YOU!

Amount Due: _____

Date Invoiced: _____

Date Due: _____

- Please make checks payable to XYZ STAGING COMPANY.
- Please mail checks to the address listed below.
- Keep this copy for your records.

Amount Paid: _____

Date Paid: _____

Services Rendered: _____

<u>Please remit to:</u>

(Your P.O Box address here)

HELPFUL HINT

I'd like to suggest that you get a P.O. Box for your business. Most of the people I've met through my business have been wonderful, but let's be realistic, it's a strange world out there and you need to protect yourself. Keep your personal address private and use your P.O. Box for business matters. They're inexpensive and you can get one at the post office near your home to make pick-ups easier.

JOB FILES

I keep a file on each job I do. This can simply mean paper clipping or stapling together all documents, notes, contracts, furniture leases, etc. pertaining to a particular job. I keep all stapled packets together in an "Active Jobs" folder, but once the job is completed, I write the date it closed and I put it into a "Completed Jobs" folder. I recommend keeping these and all other records for seven years (or whatever your tax advisor suggests).

MILEAGE

Since mileage may be a tax write off for you, be sure to keep track of yours during the year (your tax advisor can confirm this for you). At the end of every year, buy a cheap calendar and keep it in the car with a pen. When I'm going from job to job, or running a business-related errand, I can log my miles right on to the calendar. At the end of the month, I total up the mileage and make a note of it.

At the end of the year, I'll add it to all the information in my recordkeeping book and accordion file and give it to my accountant.

HIRING BUSINESS PROFESSIONALS TO ASSIST YOU

The details above describe how I manage my record-keeping. It is by no means the way you must do it. I strongly recommend you hire a small business accountant and let them advise you on the best way to keep your records. You may also want to see if the IRS is offering any free classes or advice.

HELPFUL HINT

You will probably meet many accountants once you begin networking. They will be networking the same crowd as you, and when you give them your business, they will work hard to return the favor.

Your accountant can advise you on opening a business checking account, the advisability of obtaining a business credit card, and other related banking matters.

Other professional advisors may include lawyers and insurance agents. It is critical to make sure you have personal liability insurance for when you're on the job.

INSURANCE

It is, of course, very important to have the proper insurance coverage needed before you start working in someone's home. Should you break something, valuable or otherwise, you'll want to be covered.

Speak with your own insurance supplier first to see if they offer the type of liability insurance you need. It may be a simple add-on to your existing policy. Explain that you are a home stager and need coverage in case you damage something when working in your client's home. If they can't help you, they will likely be able to suggest someone who can.

OFFICE EQUIPMENT

- Computer/printer
- Fax/photocopier/answering machine
- Telephone

In this day and age almost everyone has a computer. You can be assured that your real estate clients will. You may get requests to email invoices, contracts, or "before" and "after" pictures. If you don't have a computer, you may want to consider purchasing one and learning how to use it. Before I had my website, I was often asked to email before and after pictures. It's not hard to do, but a having a website to refer to is easier.

HELPFUL HINT

In addition to the before and after pictures you'll have on your website, you can add any other information you feel your customers would be interested in. Writing emails to your customer, sending pictures, or explaining about your business over the phone is time consuming. As a business owner, you have better things to do. Let your website do the work for you.

I find I don't use my fax machine as often as I once did, but I'm still glad I have it. They're not terribly expensive and they're nice to have when you need one. Mine has the capability to photocopy and be used as an answering machine as well. Don't buy a real cheap one, unless that's all you can afford, because if you use your fax a lot, it's necessary to have a reliable one. If your fax has poor quality, so will its other features.

HOMEWORK FOR CHAPTER 8

Call your existing insurance provider and ask about stager's insurance. You MUST get insurance. There may be other places to cut corners, but with one big, costly accident in a customer's home, you may find yourself out of business for good. *Get insurance!*

BE CREATIVE

OPPORTUNITIES EVERYWHERE

If you're promoting your business well and you can supply other services in addition to staging, you should be able to create as much work as you want or need. Just consider the huge number of real estate agents in your area. They're everywhere. If staging is not yet a widely-used service in your area, get busy educating everyone of its benefits. As with everything, you will get out of this business what you put into it.

The reality is that you have to *work* at it. You MUST network your business, get involved with realtors and other affiliates, and go to those meetings (even when you'd rather sleep in), join committees and other groups, and be involved.

Even when you're doing everything right, there will be times when your business will taper off temporarily. But even if the demand for staging has slowed down, you can focus on the other services your company provides.

The real estate market fluctuates all the time. It's different from month to month, year to year. There are times when the market is really "hot" and houses are practically selling themselves. When this happens, you may find that business slows down. If your staging company offers services other than staging, you'll be more likely to keep working.

When that hot market cools off however, you might find yourself getting quite busy. It makes sense that if there are more houses on the market, there will be greater competition to have the "best" of all the similar houses in the area. That's when staging is really in demand.

As you gain experience, you will begin to know when to expect the ups and downs of your business. For example, Thanksgiving, Christmas and the New Year holidays are typically times that home sales slow down. It's hard to sell a home during the holidays. **Don't forget to advertise "staging" for all those holiday parties**. But, try to budget your income carefully during the busy seasons and it will help get you through the slow times. That way you can relax and enjoy the holidays with everyone else.

HELPFUL HINT

Businesses, hotels, restaurants or stores in your area might enjoy some holiday "staging" in their windows, lobbies, or offices.

Opportunities are out there everywhere. You're brilliant, talented, and creative. You're loaded with all the information you need to be a huge success. What are you waiting for?

Use your imagination, and you can stage the world.

NOW, OFF YOU GO!

HOMEWORK FOR CHAPTER 9

List five other services you may be willing and/or able to provide for your customers when staging slows down:

1.

2.

3.

4.

5.

Final Thoughts

After reading all these pages, you can see that I love talking about staging. It has been the most wonderful career I could've imagined. I love being my own boss. I love making good money. But most of all, I love working at something I enjoy so much.

It is my hope that this book will help get you started on the career of *your* dreams. I want *you* to be successful. I know what it's like to struggle along not quite knowing what to do next and I know what it's like to feel intimidated by those who are more experienced. But there's no need to worry.

The advice in this book will save you months, maybe years, of valuable time—time that could be spent making your business a success rather than a series of costly mistakes. No experience? No problem! There is nothing standing in the way of you becoming a successful stager and business owner. You can do it. *I believe in you.* You're gonna be a star!

Best wishes,

Karen Kelly

APPENDIX A

(sample tool box)

When I started my staging business, I wanted to do and have everything just right. That included my tool box. In it, I have every tool known to man. But mostly I just use a hammer and nails. Once in a while I use a screw driver, a pair of scissors, or some tape. Here are some ideas for a tool box that anyone would envy.

SAMPLE TOOL BOX

Hammer
Nails (and lots of 'em)
Picture hangers that don't leave holes (check your favorite hardware store)
Screwdriver (different sizes)
Picture hooks and wire
Tape (masking, duct & regular)
Scissors
A bottle of goo remover (for taking price tags off glass, etc.)
Small jar of spackle
Apron with pockets for nails & loops for hammers & other tools
Furniture moving sliders
Box cutter
Pliers
Latex gloves
Doctor's masks
Shoulder dolly (Google "shoulder dolly" and check it out. Costs about $60.00 – need two people to use it)

I also bring cleaning supplies to each job. Here's what I've found to come in handy:

Lint brush
Carpet deodorant
Air spray (but be careful with fragrances and odors)
Windex
Paper towels
Dish towels for bigger projects (I love flour sack towels--they don't leave lint on mirrors or glass. Find them at Walmart, Target, and possibly your own grocery store)
Ajax
Sponges
Bags for trash
And once in a while, I bring an iron or steamer, if needed

APPENDIX B

(sample fliers)

STAGE IT WELL, WATCH IT SELL!®

Karen Kelly, owner/professional stager
STAGING DESIGNS

Savvy homeowners and their agents know that **staging** sells real estate! ALL homes can benefit from the services of a creative stager. From minor tweaking or de-cluttering to coordinating a moving crew and filling a home with new furniture and designer accessories, staging is an amazingly powerful selling tool.

. "We are convinced that your creativity added to the property selling the first week on the market!" – *Darron H., homeowner*

. "Thank you for staging my house so beautifully! I believe it did make a difference of around $10K in the sale price! My neighbors have said it looks so good now that my wife and I should move back in!" – *Don K., homeowner*

(Continued)

"I believe that your staging played a significant role in the client's house being the "best" of the nine that the buyer had viewed. Their offer was about $10K over the second best offer. Sure seems that the staging paid off on this listing!"– *Richard C., selling agent*

Call **Karen** today for *your* consultation!

Services provided by STAGING DESIGNS:

- Staging for the home you're about to sell
- Interior design consulting for the home you live in now
- And any home styling advice you may need (from paint colors, carpet styles, furniture and accessories selection and more.......)

Don't forget--A gift certificate for an interior design consultation makes a unique and thoughtful gift idea!

Sample Gift Certificate

THE PERFECT GIFT!

Give that special someone on your Christmas list
ONE HOUR of design time with KAREN @

STAGING DESIGNS
specializing in real estate staging and interior redesign

FOR:
a quick room redesign,
advice on color, paint, carpet, & furniture,
picking a design idea, scheme, or theme,
decorating for a holiday party or special event,
or a staging consultation for someone who may
be planning to sell their home

Call today for more information!

STAGING SELLS REAL ESTATE!

If you're a real estate agent who needs help with a listing

-or-

A homeowner who wants to sell your home faster and for more money…

I can help!

Call me today for a free consultation and staging evaluation

**Karen Kelly @
STAGING DESIGNS**

Christmas Centerpiece

For an easy, elegant Christmas centerpiece, take a collection of wine glasses, arrange them upside down on the table and use their bases as candle holders! Place a pillar-style candle on the base of each glass. For added interest, use mismatched glasses of varying heights. Around the glasses, add some pine branches, apples, walnuts and berries for a festive, holiday arrangement!

For other great decorating tips and ideas, contact:

STAGING DESIGNS by Karen Kelly

S.T.A.G.E. It Well

Spaciousness

Your goal is to make all the rooms in your home look large, airy, and spacious.

Tidiness

Everything should be clean and sparkling--windows, floors, countertops, baseboards, etc. Much can be forgiven if your house is sparkling clean.

Accessorize

Artwork, simple tabletop decorations, and greenery are all important details that will help a buyer connect with your home in a positive way.

Generalize:

Your home should appeal to as many people as possible. De-personalize your space by eliminating family, cultural, or religious items, artwork, and decorations.

Eleven Seconds

That's about how long you've got to make a great first impression. It's not much time, so you've really got to make it count!

Call Karen @ Staging Designs for more staging details and ideas.

Dear Reader: Please join me for one of my

New-Stager Training Workshops

Visit my website for class information.

If you'd like to schedule a training session in your area, contact me today for availability, course details, and pricing.

"Before I met Karen, I had started my staging business a year prior. I had a few staging jobs under my belt; however I still felt a little inexperienced and lacked a lot of confidence. I'm so thankful and fortunate to have gone through Karen's training. She helped me learn more about staging techniques, the tools needed and other great suggestions for the back end of the business such as administration and contracts. I not only have a great mentor, but a wonderful friend that is always there to help!"-Lilly Rahbar from Simplistic Staging by LJR

www.stageitwell.com